# BRANCH LINES TO LAUNCESTON AND PRINCETOWN

**Vic Mitchell and Keith Smith**

Middleton Press

Cover photograph: An autotrain shelters under the welcoming roof of Tavistock South station on 23rd June 1962, while 2-6-2T no. 5544 runs south with local freight. This was the last Summer for passengers to enjoy the branch. (M.J.Messenger)

Published July 1998

ISBN 1 901706 19 2

© Middleton Press

Design Deborah Goodridge

Published by
        Middleton Press
        Easebourne Lane
        Midhurst, West Sussex
        GU29 9AZ
Tel: 01730 813169
Fax: 01730 812601

Printed & bound by Biddles Ltd,
        Guildford and Kings Lynn

# CONTENTS

# ACKNOWLEDGEMENTS

In addition to the photographers mentioned in the credits, we would like to express our appreciation of the assistance received from P.G.Barnes, A.E.Bennett, G.Croughton, D.Cullum, K.Greenwood, Mrs S.Grove, T.Heavyside, F.Hornby, M.King, J.R.W.Kirkby, N.Langridge, P.Mitchell, Mr D. & Dr S.Salter, N.Sprinks, C.P.Stacey, E.Youldon and our ever helpful wives.

October 1905

## PRINCETOWN, TAVISTOCK AND LAUNCESTON.

| | Week Days | | | | | | | | | | | | | | | | | Sundays | | | |
|---|---|---|---|---|---|---|---|---|---|---|---|---|---|---|---|---|---|---|---|---|---|
| | a.m. | a.m. | a.m. | a.m. | | a.m. | p.m. | | | p.m. | | | p.m. | p.m. | p.m. | p.m. | p.m. | p.m. | a.m. | a.m. | p.m. | p.m. |
| Plymouth {Millbay dep | 7 0 | 7 35 | 8 40 | 10 15 | | 11 50 | 12 2 | | | 2 5 | | | 3 10 | 4 27 | 5 10 | 6 7 | 650 | 945 | 1055 | 9 35 | 11 0 | 2 0 | 910 |
| N'th Rd. ,, | 7 4 | 7 39 | 8 45 | 10 22 | | 11 57 | 2 9 | | | 2 9 | | | 3 15 | 4 30 | 5 14 | 6 11 | 654 | 949 | 11 0 | 9 39 | 11 3 | 2 4 | 914 |
| Mutley ,, | 7 6 | 7 41 | 8 46 | 10 25 | | 12 0 | 12 6 | | | 2 10 | | | 3 18 | 4 32 | 5 16 | 6 13 | 657 | 951 | 11 0 | 9 41 | 11 4 | 2 7 | 916 |
| Marsh Mills ,, | 7 13 | 7 48 | 8 55 | 10 32 | | 12 7 | 12 15 | | | 2 20 | | | 3 26 | 4 41 | 5 23 | 6 20 | 7 4 | 958 | 11 10 | 9 48 | 1118 | 213 | 923 |
| Bickleigh ,, | 7 22 | 7 50 | 9 6 | 10 43 | | 12 10 | | M | | 2 33 | | | 3 35 | | 5 33 | 6 31 | 715 | 10 0 | 1122 | 9 50 | 1123 | 221 | 931 |
| Yelverton ,, | 7 33 | 8 11 | 9 17 | 10 53 | | 12 31 | | M | | 2 47 | | | 3 51 | M | 5 45 | 6 42 | 729 | 1026 | 1132 | 10 10 | 1133 | 234 | 945 |
| Yelverton dep | | 8 48 | | 11 10 | | 12 15 | | | | 3 5 | | | | | | | 742 | | | | | 245 | |
| Dousland ,, | | 8 54 | | 11 16 | | 12 21 | | | | 3 11 | | | | | | | 748 | | | | M | 251 | |
| Princetown arr | | 9 24 | | 11 43 | | 12 48 | | | | 3 35 | | | | | | | 8 15 | | | | | 318 | |
| Horrabridge dep | | 8 16 | 9 22 | 11 2 | | 12 36 | | | 2 55 | | | 3 57 | | | 5 50 | 647 | 735 | 1025 | 1136 | 10 15 | 1157 | | 9 50 |
| Tavistock ,, | | 8 22 | 9 30 | 11 12 | | 12 49 | | | 3 3 | | | 4 8 | | | 5 59 | 657 | 743 | 1038 | 1145 | 1025 | 1145 | | 10 0 |
| Marytavy ,, | | 8 36 | | | | 12 59 | | | | | | 4 10 | | | 6 37 | | 754 | | | 1034 | | | 10 9 |
| Lydford ,, | | 8 45 | | | | 1 8 | | | | | | 4 27 | | | 6 44 | | 8 3 | | | 1043 | | | 1018 |
| Coryton ,, | | 8 55 | | | | 1 20 | | | | | | 4 38 | | | 6 51 | | 815 | | | 1053 | | | 1028 |
| Lifton ,, | | 9 3 | | | | 1 29 | | | | | | 6 48 | | | 6 54 | | 822 | | | 11 1 | | | 1036 |
| Launceston arr | | 9 13 | | | | 1 40 | | | | | | 4 55 | | | 6 54 | | 832 | | | 1111 | | | 1046 |

| | | a.m. | a.m. | a.m. | | p.m. | p.m. | p.m. | p.m. | p.m. | | p.m. | | p.m. | | p.m. | p.m. | p.m. | | a.m. | a.m. | p.m. | p.m. |
|---|---|---|---|---|---|---|---|---|---|---|---|---|---|---|---|---|---|---|---|---|---|---|---|
| Launceston dep | | 7 35 | | | | | | | | | | 6 20 | | 8 15 | | | 7 40 | | | | 6 30 | | | |
| Lifton ,, | | 7 45 | 10 1 | | | | 2 0 | | | | | 6 31 | | 8 24 | | | 7 50 | | | | 6 40 | | | |
| Coryton ,, | | 7 55 | 10 9 | | | | 2 16 | | | | | 6 39 | | 8 32 | | | 7 58 | M | | | 6 48 | | | |
| Lydford ,, | | 8 7 | 10 25 | | | | 2 29 | | | | | 6 52 | | 8 40 | | | 8 11 | | | | 7 1 | | | |
| Marytavy ,, | | 8 15 | 10 33 | | | | 2 36 | | | | | 7 0 | | 8 51 | | | 8 19 | | | | 7 9 | | | |
| Tavistock ,, | | 8 26 | 9 45 | 10 41 | | 12 55 | 2 43 | | 4 50 | | | 7 10 | | 7 45 | | | 9 5 | 1045 | 1155 | | 8 28 | 1155 | | 718 |
| Horrabridge ,, | | 8 35 | 9 55 | 10 51 | | 1 5 | 2 56 | | 5 0 | | | 7 20 | | 7 55 | | | 9 15 | 1055 | 12 5 | | 8 38 | 12 4 | | 725 |
| Princetown dep | 7 10 | 7 55 | | 10 17 | | 12 52 | 2 10 | | | | | 6 45 | | | | | | | | | | | 5 15 | |
| Dousland ,, | 7 35 | 8 15 | | 10 45 | | 1 0 | 2 38 | | | | | 7 13 | | | | | | | | | | | 543 | |
| Yelverton arr | 7 43 | 8 18 | | 10 50 | | 1 5 | 2 43 | | | | | 7 18 | | | | | | | | | | | 548 | |
| Yelverton dep | 7 50 | 8 40 | 10 | 10 57 | | 1 10 | | | | 5 5 | | 7 26 | | 8 0 | | | 9 20 | 11 0 | 1210 | | 8 44 | 12 8 | 6 0 | 733 |
| Bickleigh ,, | 8 1 | 8 47 | 10 | 11 5 | | M | 118 | 3 9 | M | 513 | | 7 44 | | 8 10 | | | 10 28 | 11 8 | 1218 | | 852 | 1215 | 6 8 | 741 |
| Marsh Mills ,, | 8 10 | 8 55 | 10 16 | 11 14 | | 1220 | 126 | 3 17 | 5 5 | 524 | | 7 44 | | 8 16 | | | 9 38 | 1117 | 1227 | | 9 1 | 1221 | 616 | 750 |
| Plymouth {Mutley arr | 8 16 | 9 0 | 10 22 | 11 21 | | 1230 | 132 | 3 23 | 515 | 531 | | 7 50 | | 8 23 | | | 9 44 | 1123 | 1233 | | 9 7 | 1233 | 622 | 756 |
| N'th Rd. ,, | 8 18 | 9 2 | 1025 | 11 24 | | 1229 | 139 | 3 26 | 517 | 535 | | 7 53 | | 8 25 | | | 9 47 | 1125 | 1235 | | 910 | 1235 | 624 | 756 |
| Millbay ,, | 8 23 | 9 8 | 1032 | 11 30 | | 1235 | 140 | 3 33 | 521 | 540 | | 7 50 | | 8 30 | | | 9 51 | 1130 | 1240 | | 915 | 1238 | 630 | 8 4 |

D Mixed Train.
L Tuesdays excepted.
M Rail Motor Car, one Class only.
S Saturdays only.

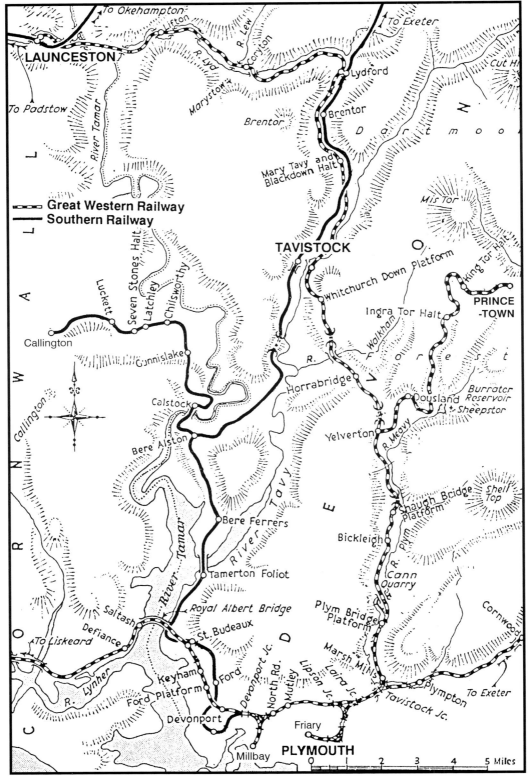

Passenger railways 1935-40 (Railway Magazine)

# GEOGRAPHICAL SETTING

## Plymouth to Launceston

The route from Plymouth to Launceston followed the steep-sided valley of the River Plym for five miles and then ran close to the River Meavy to Yelverton. The surrounding land was mainly Carboniferous and Devonian slates for the entire line.

High ground was crossed before joining the River Walkham and following it downstream for about one mile. A further climb and descent took the line to Tavistock where it joined the Tavy Valley. It ran close to the Tavy for about two miles and then accompanied a tributary, the small River Burn, northwards to Lydford.

Here it joined the west flowing River Lyd and ran close to it to within about two miles of Launceston. For the first mile it was near the River Tamar and the final length into this market town was in the company of the east-flowing River Kensey. Most of the route was in Devon, only this final length being in Cornwall.

## Princetown branch

This steeply graded line started on the Devonian Slates and reached the Granite of Dartmoor near Peek Hill, east of Walkhampton.

# HISTORICAL BACKGROUND

The Plymouth & Dartmoor Railway, the first in the area, was authorised under an Act of 2nd July 1819. Further Acts in 1820 and 1821 gave a total mileage of twenty five and a half. The main purpose of this 4ft 6ins gauge line was the conveyance of timber, lime and other building materials from Plymouth to a new prison under construction near Pprincetown. It was to house prisoners from the Napoleonic Wars. The route from Sutton Pool to King's Tor was opened on 26th September 1823 and was horse-worked.

The line fell into disuse in the 1840s, the northern part eventually becoming part of the Princetown branch. The Lee Moor Tramway on Dartmoor was connected to a branch of the southern section in 1856 for the conveyance of china clay, traffic being destined to Laira Wharf, below Laira Bridge.The line remained in use (for gravel, but still horse operated) south to Maddocks Concrete Works at the south end of Laira Yard until October 1960.

The first main line in the district was that of the South Devon Railway which arrived at Plymouth (Laira Green) on 5th May 1848 and was built to the broad gauge of seven foot and one quarter inch. It was extended to Plymouth Millbay on 2nd April 1849.

The Tavistock & South Devon Railway's Act was passed on 24th July 1854 and the line opened on 22nd June 1859. The Launceston & South Devon Railway Act followed on 30th June 1862, trains commencing on 1st July 1865. All services were provided by the SDR and all three companies had become part of the Great Western Railway by 1878.

The London & South Western Railway had long had Plymouth as its goal. Its line from Okehampton to Lydford opened on 12th October 1874 and its trains continued to Plymouth via the route featured in this album. A third rail was laid for their standard gauge trains.

A branch to Princetown was authorised on 13th August 1878 and opened on 11th August 1883. It was built by the Princetown Railway to standard gauge and was operated by the GWR.

The LSWR continued to use their rival's tracks until 2nd June 1890 when they obtained the use of an independent route between Lydford and Plymouth via Bere Alston. The LSWR had provided further competition for the GWR when it reached Launceston on 21st July 1886. The line was extended west to Tresmeer on 21st July 1892. The other broad gauge lines of the area received an additional rail to accommodate standard gauge trains from 17th May 1876. Broad gauge traffic ceased on 20th May 1892.

The LSWR became part of the Southern Railway in 1923. Upon nationalisation in 1948, the SR lines in the area formed part of the Southern Region, while the GWR routes were put into the Western Region.

The maps are to the scale of 25 ins to 1 mile and north is at the top, unless otherwise noted.

## Closures

Total closure of the Princetown branch occurred on 5th March 1956. Passenger services between Plymouth and Launceston were withdrawn after 31st December 1962, but freight continued to be handled at some stations, details being given in the captions.

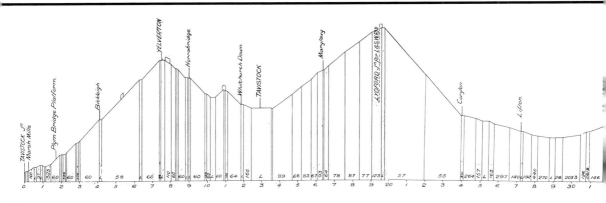

# PASSENGER SERVICES

The initial service to Tavistock comprised five trains on weekdays and four on Sundays. The latter was soon halved. The same frequency was maintained when operations were extended to Launceston.

From 1874, there were an addtional seven weekday trains provided by the LSWR south of Lydford, with one on Sundays which was soon withdrawn. They all stopped at all stations.

The table indicates the number of departures for Plymouth daily but it does not include those trains running on selected weekdays only.

|  | From Tavistock | | From Launceston | | From Princetown | |
|---|---|---|---|---|---|---|
|  | Weekdays | Sundays | Weekdays | Sundays | Weekdays | Sundays |
| 1889 | 13 | 4 | 5 | 2 | 3 | 0 |
| 1911 | 12 | 3 | 5 | 2 | 6 | 1 |
| 1931 | 14 | 3 | 4 | 0 | 4 | 0 |
| 1951 | 9 | 3 | 4 | 0 | 6 | 0 |
| 1961 | 8 | 0 | 3 | 0 | - | - |

All Sunday trains were withdrawn in 1958

## Princetown branch

Four or five trains on weekdays, with an extra one on some Saturdays and other days, was usual throughout the life of the line. In a few of the early years, there were two trains on Sundays in the Summer months.

## PLYMOUTH, TAVISTOCK, and LAUNCESTON.—Great Western.

| Mls | Down. | mrn | mrn | aft | aft | aft | | mrn | aft | Mls | Up. | mrn | mrn | aft | aft | aft | | mrn | aft |
|---|---|---|---|---|---|---|---|---|---|---|---|---|---|---|---|---|---|---|---|
| — | Plymouth, Millbay | 8 23 | 1117 | 2 35 | 5 55 | 8 35 | | 9 35 | 8 35 | — | Launceston ..dep | 7 40 | 1030 | 2 5 | 6 | 8 10 | | 7 40 | 6 10 |
| ¼ | " North Road | 8 28 | 1123 | 2 41 | 6 | 8 39 | | 9 39 | 8 39 | 4¼ | Lifton | 7 49 | 1039 | 2 14 | 6 14 | 8 19 | | 7 49 | 6 19 |
| 1 | " Mutley | 8 30 | 1126 | 2 44 | 6 | 8 41 | | 9 41 | 8 41 | 8 | Coryton | 7 58 | 1049 | 2 23 | 6 23 | 8 27 | | 7 58 | 6 27 |
| 4 | Marsh Mills | 8 38 | 1133 | 2 51 | 6 13 | 8 50 | | 9 48 | 8 47 | 12½ | Lidford 51 | 8 11 | 11 2 | 2 36 | 6 36 | 8 40 | | 8 11 | 6 40 |
| 7½ | Bickleigh | 8 53 | 1146 | 3 | 6 24 | 9 3 | | 9 59 | 8 58 | 15½ | Mary Tavy | 8 19 | 1112 | 2 47 | 6 44 | 8 48 | | 8 19 | 6 48 |
| 11½ | Yelverton 14 | 9 3 | 1158 | 3 14 | 6 35 | 9 13 | | 1010 | 9 9 | 19 | Tavistock | 8 28 | 1121 | 2 56 | 6 53 | 8 57 | | 8 28 | 6 57 |
| 12½ | Horrabridge | 9 12 | 4 3 | 206 | 40 | 9 18 | | 1015 | 9 16 | 23 | Horrabridge | 8 40 | 1131 | 3 7 | 7 3 | 9 7 | | 8 35 | 7 7 |
| 16½ | Tavistock | 9 18 | 1216 | 3 30 | 6 52 | 9 29 | | 1026 | 9 27 | 24½ | Yelverton 14 | 8 45 | 1136 | 3 15 | 7 13 | 9 13 | | 8 44 | 7 12 |
| 20 | Mary Tavy | 9 28 | 1225 | 3 39 | 7 1 | 9 38 | | 1035 | 9 36 | 27½ | Bickleigh | 8 53 | 1145 | 3 25 | 7 24 | 9 15 | | 8 52 | 7 21 |
| 23½ | Lidford 51 | 9 37 | 1235 | 3 49 | 7 10 | 9 46 | | 1043 | 9 44 | 31¼ | Marsh Mills | 9 2 | 1153 | 3 35 | 7 34 | 9 30 | | 9 1 | 7 31 |
| 27½ | Coryton | 9 47 | 1245 | 3 59 | 7 21 | 9 56 | | 1053 | 9 55 | 34¼ | Plymouth, Mutley | 9 8 | 12 2 | 3 42 | 7 41 | 9 36 | | 9 7 | 7 37 |
| 30½ | Lifton | 9 54 | 1252 | 4 7 | 7 29 | 10 4 | | 11 1 | 10 4 | 34½ | " North Road | 9 10 | 12 3 | 3 44 | 7 43 | 9 38 | | 9 10 | 7 40 |
| 35½ | Launceston 51 arr | 10 5 | 1 4 | 4 18 | 7 40 | 1016 | | 1112 | 1014 | 35½ | " Millbay 18 a | 9 15 | 1210 | 3 51 | 7 50 | 9 44 | | 9 15 | 7 45 |

*SUNDAYS.*

May 1889

October 1911

## PLYMOUTH, YELVERTON, PRINCETOWN, TAVISTOCK, and LAUNCESTON.—Great Western.

*Week Days. Sundays. NOTES.*

### LAUNCESTON, TAVISTOCK SOUTH, PRINCETOWN and PLYMOUTH

*Week Days. Suns.*

**A** 1 mile to Tavistock North.   **Ä** Arr. 10 15 p.m.   **D** Commences 18th March   **K** Tuesdays, Thursdays and Saturdays.   **S** Saturdays only.   **Ü** Arr. 4 mins *earlier*   **Ø** Third class only.   **W** Train temporarily withdrawn

March 1951

# PLYMOUTH MILLBAY

Initially the terminus for trains from the east, the station became the terminus for services from the west also, when the Cornwall Railway was completed in 1859. Known as the "Cornwall Loop", a direct connection between the two routes was opened in 1876, this forming the triangular junction shown on the left. South of the station are the lines to Millbay Docks which were used by boat trains connecting with liners until the 1960s. Until 1941, our journey to Launceston could have started at Millbay station (left centre) and continued via North Road (upper centre) and Mutley (top right). This 1938 map is at the scale of six inches to one mile.

1. The centre two of the four platforms were used by long distance trains, numbers 1 and 4 generally receiving local services in the early years. The engine release crossover is evident in this 1913 photograph and also in the next one. (LGRP/NRM)

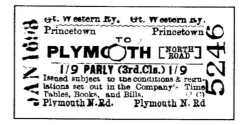

K<sup>800</sup>8358
2d

DEFIANCE
SALTASH
St. Budeaux
KEYHAM
Dockyard H'lt
FORD
Devonport
Wingfield Villas Halt
PLYMOUTH (Millbay)
MUTLEY
Lipson Vale Halt
LAIRA HALT
Marsh Mills
Plym Bridge Halt
Plympton

GREAT WESTERN RLY.
RAIL-MOTOR CARS.

Williamson, Printer, Ashton

Gt. Western Ry.     Gt. Western Ry.
Princetown          Princetown
           TO
PLYMOUTH [NORTH ROAD]
1/9 PARLY (3rd.Cls.) 1/9
Issued subject to the conditions & regulations set out in the Company's Time Tables, Books, and Bills.
Plymouth N.Rd.     Plymouth N. Rd

JAN 16 38

5246

2. An autotrain was recorded at platform 3 sometime in the 1930s. The station suffered severe bomb damage on 23rd April 1941 and passenger services ceased, never to be reinstated. (Stations UK)

4. New buildings were erected in 1900 and were photographed in 1970. The platforms were removed in 1959 to make space for more berthing sidings. (Stations UK)

3. Following closure, the station and adjacent sidings were used for carriage berthing and servicing. Empty stock for the Tavistock route is leaving behind 0-4-2T no. 1434 on 12th July 1955, while window washing proceeds at the disused platform 4. (R.C.Riley)

**Other views of the station and docks can be found in *Branch Lines around Plymouth*, pictures 3 to 15.**

# PLYMOUTH NORTH ROAD

5. The station did not open until 28th March 1877 and was built by the GWR as a result of pressure from the LSWR, whose trains could not stop near the centre of Plymouth. There were only two platforms at the joint station until 1908. This westward view is probably from the 1930s. (Lens of Sutton)

6. Looking east, we see one of the four through lines, two of which had two platforms each, as shown. LSWR trains from London called at the station in the opposite direction to GWR trains after the former's new terminus at Plymouth Friary was opened in 1890. (Lens of Sutton)

7. On the left is the east end of the old station and the 1939 East Box. The locomotive featured is no. 6009 *King Charles II*. Rebuilding of the unsatisfactory station commenced in 1938, was delayed by the war, restarted in 1956 and was completed in 1962, the year in which trains on our route ceased. (J.G.Sturt)

**More pictures of Plymouth North Road and Mutley can be found in our *Tavistock to Plymouth* album. They are numbered 99 to 109.**

# MUTLEY

8. This station served a residential area of Plymouth and was opened before North Road, on 1st August 1871. It had both LSWR and GWR booking offices after 1874; the signal box (centre) closed in 1896. In this eastward postcard view, smoke emerges from the 183yd long Mutley Tunnel. Further east, Lipson Vale Halt was in use from 1st June 1904 to 22nd March 1942. (Lens of Sutton)

# LAIRA

(below)
9. At the west end of the Laira complex was Lipson Junction. The curve to Plymouth Friary is on the left as "Castle" class no. 5069 *Isambard Kingdom Brunel* accelerates an up express on 30th August 1961. The box was in use from 1891 to 1960. (R.C.Riley)

10. In the distance is the signal box seen in the picture below, while on the left is part of the massive Laira Engine Shed, which was in use from 1906 to 1965. Laira Halt was opened on 1st June 1904 and closed on 7th July 1930. (Lens of Sutton)

11. Laira shed is in the background as the up "Royal Duchy" passes Laira Junction box, headed by no. 6016 *King Edward V*. Most of the marshalling yard is beyond the left border of the photograph, which is from the 1950s. The box was in use from 1903 until 1973. Crossing the main lines diagonally is the 4ft 6ins gauge Lee Moor Tramway; the track is boarded for the benefit of the horses used for haulage. (R.C.Riley)

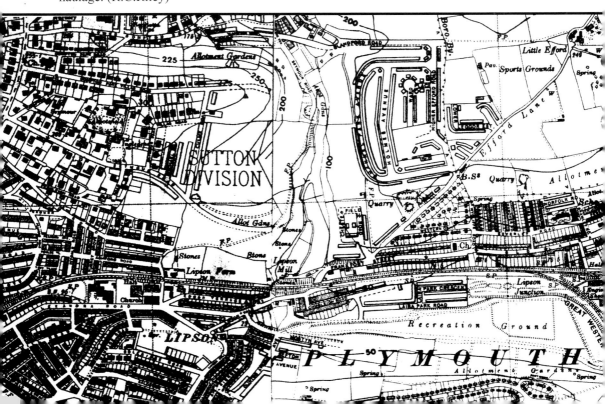

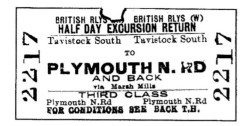

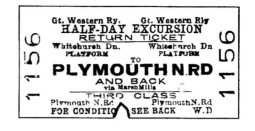

This map is a continuation of the previous one and shows Lipson Vale Halt on the left, Laira Halt left of centre and Marsh Mills on the right. Trains to Plymouth Friary, Turnchapel and Yealmpton took the line at the bottom - see *Branch Lines around Plymouth*. The line to Exeter is on the right.

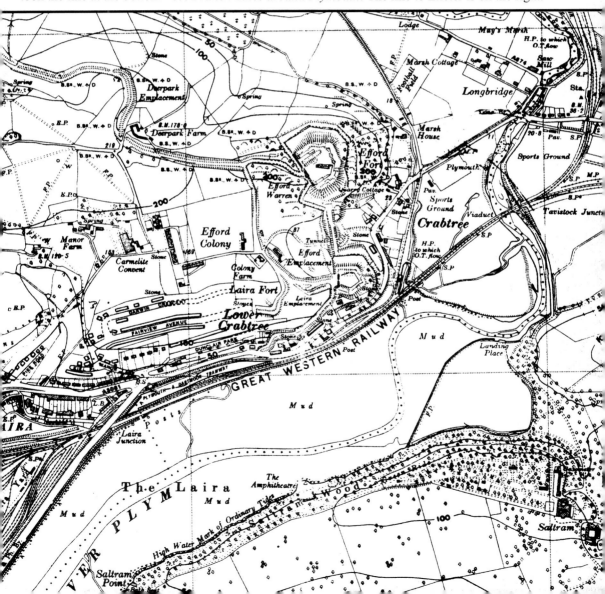

12. The previous photograph was taken from the bridge on the left. The Lee Moor Tramway was closed and overgrown when photographed in June 1962, but the two ringed signals protecting its level crossing were still to be seen adjacent to the track. The gates were worked by a wheel in the signal box. (J.J.Smith)

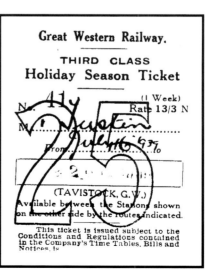

Great Western Railway.

THIRD CLASS
Holiday Season Ticket

(1 Week)
N. 41y                                    Rate 13/3 N

From............................to............

(TAVISTOCK, G.W.)
Available between the Stations shown
on the other side by the routes indicated.

This ticket is issued subject to the
Conditions and Regulations contained
in the Company's Time Tables, Bills and
Notices, is

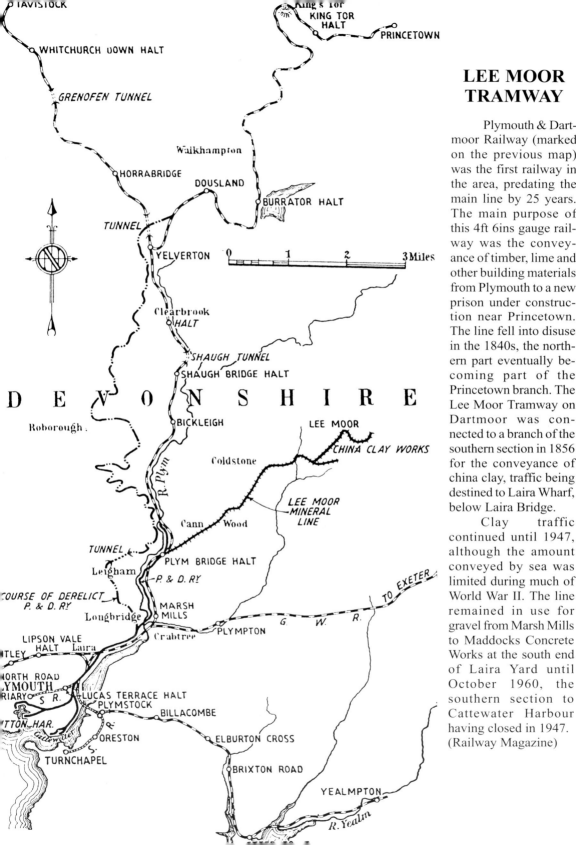

## LEE MOOR TRAMWAY

Plymouth & Dartmoor Railway (marked on the previous map) was the first railway in the area, predating the main line by 25 years. The main purpose of this 4ft 6ins gauge railway was the conveyance of timber, lime and other building materials from Plymouth to a new prison under construction near Princetown. The line fell into disuse in the 1840s, the northern part eventually becoming part of the Princetown branch. The Lee Moor Tramway on Dartmoor was connected to a branch of the southern section in 1856 for the conveyance of china clay, traffic being destined to Laira Wharf, below Laira Bridge.

Clay traffic continued until 1947, although the amount conveyed by sea was limited during much of World War II. The line remained in use for gravel from Marsh Mills to Maddocks Concrete Works at the south end of Laira Yard until October 1960, the southern section to Cattewater Harbour having closed in 1947. (Railway Magazine)

13. Roadside running near Laira was recorded in 1928, five wagons being the maximum load for two horses. (R.S.Carpenter coll.)

14. The line crossed the River Plym at Weighbridge Cottage; this is marked on the next map. Here we look east over the bridge, Marsh Mills station being hidden by the trees. The bridge and cottage were still to be seen in 1998. (R.S.Carpenter coll.)

15. About one mile from Tavistock Junction, the LMT crossed the Launceston branch on the level. This is a view towards Marsh Mills in 1922; the signal box was closed in January 1955, having earlier served as "A" (North) Box at Tavistock. (R.M.Casserley coll.)

16. Cann Wood Incline had a passing place at its mid-point and was photographed in 1922, looking east. Torycombe Incline was near the end of the line, close to Lee Moor China Clay Works. (F.H.C.Casbourn/SLS)

17. Between the two inclines was a two-mile long section of track sufficiently level for locomotive working and two Peckett 0-4-0ST ran on it between 1899 and 1947, when the LMT was closed north of Marsh Mills. Both engines are preserved. (R.S.Carpenter coll.)

18. The locomotive shed (left) and fitters shop at Lee Moor were photographed in 1960. China clay had been conveyed to Marsh Mills by pipeline since 1947. The southern part of the route is illustrated in *Tavistock to Plymouth* (no. 111) and picture nos 28 to 40 and 59 in *Branch Lines around Plymouth*. (H.Davies coll.)

19. Tavistock Junction is the point at which the Launceston branch (centre) diverged from the Exeter line (right). It is on the right of the map. There were 25 sidings in the angle of the junction. (L.W.Crosier)

20. The line from Marsh Mills (foreground) was diverted on 27th June 1965 to join the end of no. 4 siding, seen near the shed in the previous picture. Sidings 5 to 13 had to be shortened to accommodate the curve seen here as no. 09008 hauls empties northwards on 24th October 1997. (D.H.Mitchell)

21. The same locomotive runs towards the main line connection on 29th April 1997 with one Cargowagon containing bagged china clay from Marsh Mills. Track maintenance machines are housed on the right. (D.H.Mitchell)

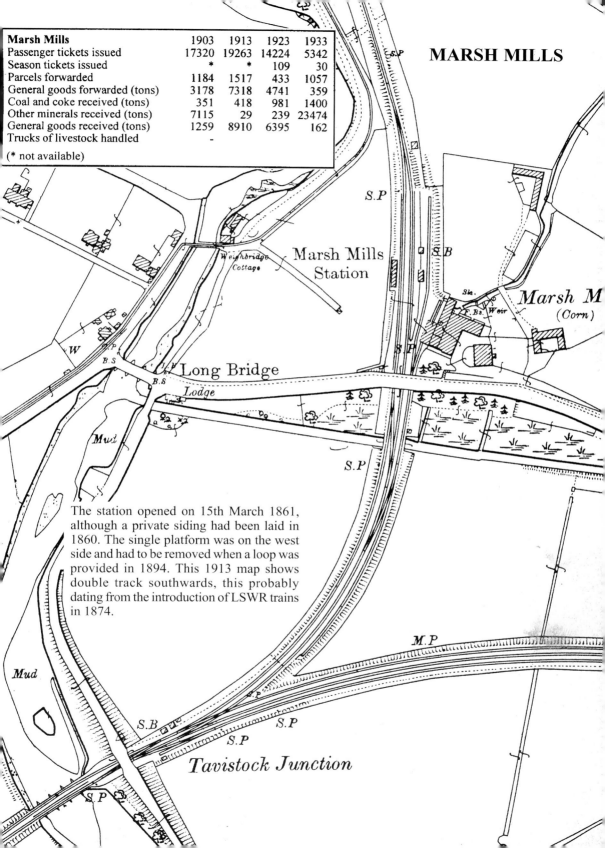

| Marsh Mills | 1903 | 1913 | 1923 | 1933 |
|---|---|---|---|---|
| Passenger tickets issued | 17320 | 19263 | 14224 | 5342 |
| Season tickets issued | * | * | 109 | 30 |
| Parcels forwarded | 1184 | 1517 | 433 | 1057 |
| General goods forwarded (tons) | 3178 | 7318 | 4741 | 359 |
| Coal and coke received (tons) | 351 | 418 | 981 | 1400 |
| Other minerals received (tons) | 7115 | 29 | 239 | 23474 |
| General goods received (tons) | 1259 | 8910 | 6395 | 162 |
| Trucks of livestock handled | - | | | |

(* not available)

*Weighbridge Cottage*

Marsh Mills
Station

*S.P*

*S.B*

Marsh M
(Corn)

*Sta.*

*F.Bs*  *Weir*

*W*

*B.S*

Long Bridge

*B.S*

*Lodge*

*Mud*

*S.P*

The station opened on 15th March 1861, although a private siding had been laid in 1860. The single platform was on the west side and had to be removed when a loop was provided in 1894. This 1913 map shows double track southwards, this probably dating from the introduction of LSWR trains in 1874.

*Mud*

*M.P*

*S.B*

*S.P*

*S.P*

Tavistock Junction

*S.P*

22. The crew of 0-6-0PT no. 6400 are about to surrender the token as they pass the 1894 signal box, which was given a new 32-lever frame in 1919. Trains to Launceston were termed "down" trains. (M.Daly)

23. A view from the bridge seen in the previous picture features 2-6-2T no. 5572 propelling an autocoach of a late design on 17th March 1962. The siding nearest the fence was of an early date; the other two were added in 1932 and served a tarmacadam plant. (M.J.Messenger)

24. The Plymouth Railway Circle arranged a tour on 18th June 1966. No. D2178 was recorded at the long disused down platform with its train of brake vans for the happy enthusiasts. (M.J.Messenger)

25. Loaded wagons from the nearby clay dries pass the remains of the down platform on 24th October 1997, hauled by no. 09008. The centre line of the track was close to that of the point rodding seen in the earlier pictures. (D.H.Mitchell)

# PLYM VALLEY RAILWAY

26. The group was formed in 1980 and some track was laid on the old route of the Launceston branch in 1989. The railway has been a temporary home for many locomotives subsequently, including this 3ft 6ins gauge ex-South African Railways Garratt no. 4112 *Springbok* of 1957, photographed in 1984. (C.L.Caddy)

27. Ex-Falmouth Docks 1926 Hawthorn Leslie 0-4-0ST no. 3 was demonstrating freight shunting at North Junction on 22nd June 1997. On the right is ex-BR class 08 no. 13002. Plans were made to operate a passenger service in 1998 over the quarter of a mile of track south to the station shown in the next picture. (B.Mills)

28. A January 1998 photograph shows the platform under construction, about 200yds north of the original station site. Undergoing restoration on the left is BR class 4 4-6-0 no. 75079. The stones from Billacombe station awaited re-erection here. Also on site in 1998 was a class 117 2-car DMU, together with two industrial diesels, three coaches, two brake vans and 15 wagons. (B.Mills)

29. The Dartmoor China Clay Company laid sidings east of the GWR branch in 1919. They became the property of English China Clays, Lovering, Pochin & Co Ltd in 1951; their 1940 Fowler 0-4-0 diesel is seen at work on 15th June 1957, adjacent to their power station. (M.Dart)

30. Their fireless Bagnall locomotive was recorded on 9th August 1967. Regular visits to the steam supply from the power station were necessary, as seen. It is standing at the same location as the previous picture. The locomotive was stored at Bodmin Parkway in 1998, awaiting restoration. (M.Dart)

31. The clay output was being loaded into CDA wagons which are being hauled through the shed on 23rd July 1997 by no. 09008. The Army's Coypool sidings were west of the GWR line from 1941 until about 1980. (M.Dart)

# PLYM BRIDGE PLATFORM

32. A timber platform was opened on 1st May 1906 and much used by walkers and picnickers at weekends. It was rebuilt in concrete in 1949 but at a shorter length. Early morning and evening trains were not scheduled to stop, due to the lack of lighting. (R.M.Casserley coll.)

# SOUTH OF BICKLEIGH

33. The Cann Quarry branch of the Plymouth & Dartmoor Railway passed under the line north of Plym Bridge Platform and then back under it again at Cann Viaduct to reach Cann Quarry. The original timber structure was replaced by this six-arch stone viaduct in 1907. (M.Dart coll.)

34. Riverford Viaduct comprised five granite arches after rebuilding from timber in 1893. No. 4570 is working the 3.5pm from Plymouth North Road to Launceston on 4th August 1962. (S.C.Nash)

35. Running south on the same day on Bickleigh Viaduct is no. 5544, with freight from Launceston. Also evident is part of Dartmoor and Bickleigh fixed distant signal. The seven stone arches date from 1893. (S.C.Nash)

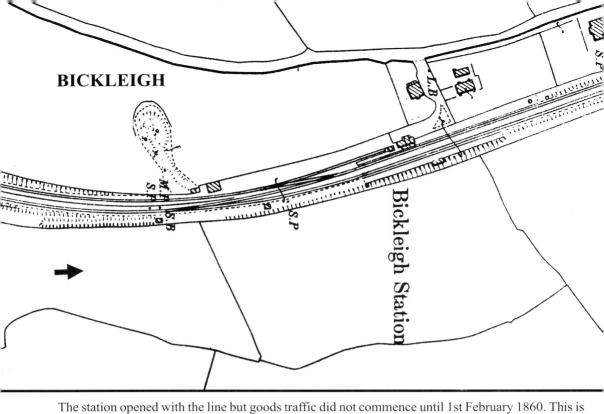

BICKLEIGH

Bickleigh Station

The station opened with the line but goods traffic did not commence until 1st February 1860. This is the 1906 edition.

36. A southward view in 1961 emphasises the rural location of the station, it being another popular destination for hikers. The wide space between the tracks was a legacy from the broad gauge days. (R.C.Riley)

37. One coach sufficed for the Launceston service, in terminal decline on 15th July 1961. The signal box remained in use until the end. Note that this was an intermediate watering point for locomotives. (R.C.Riley)

38. No. 4567 was working the 10.15 from Launceston on 4th August 1962. The point rods ran northwards in the "six-foot" but southwards adjacent to the platform, probably because they were fewer. (S.C.Nash)

39. The signal box (right) was built in 1913 and had a 23-lever frame. The previous box had been demolished to allow southward extension of the loop. The one prior to that is on the left, having for long served as a goods shed. The photograph was taken in March 1964. Only the station house and part of the platform remained in 1998. (C.L.Caddy)

# SHAUGH BRIDGE PLATFORM

40. The platform was built on the east side of the line and was opened on 29th October 1928. It was north of the six-arch Ham Green Viaduct, which had been of timber construction until 1899. Autotrains for ramblers terminated here for many Summers before World War II. The platform extended under the road bridge from which these photographs were taken. (Lens of Sutton)

41. Taken a few weeks before closure, this photograph includes the effects of nature on the lineside, and 2-6-2T no. 4555. Built in 1924, this locomotive avoided the scrapman and now can be seen on the Paignton & Dartmouth Steam Railway. Further north is the 307yd long Shaugh Tunnel, near which was a siding for iron ore in about 1870-74. (R.C.Riley)

# CLEARBROOK HALT

42. Passenger services commenced here on 29th October 1928, the scenic attractions generating most of the traffic. The halt also served the residents of nearby Hoo Meavy and Goodameavy. No. 4583 is northbound on 21st August 1947 and obscures the arc-roofed waiting shelter. (R.J.Buckley)

| Bickleigh | 1903 | 1913 | 1923 | 1933 |
|---|---|---|---|---|
| Passenger tickets issued | 10331 | 12794 | 12304 | 9685 |
| Season tickets issued | * | * | 100 | 74 |
| Parcels forwarded | 1071 | 1643 | 1931 | 681 |
| General goods forwarded (tons) | 75 | 42 | 43 | 42 |
| Coal and coke received (tons) | 506 | 676 | 400 | 550 |
| Other minerals received (tons) | 1013 | 323 | 672 | 1224 |
| General goods received (tons) | 89 | 779 | 481 | 62 |
| Trucks of livestock handled | - | 18 | 43 | 24 |
| (* not available) | | | | |

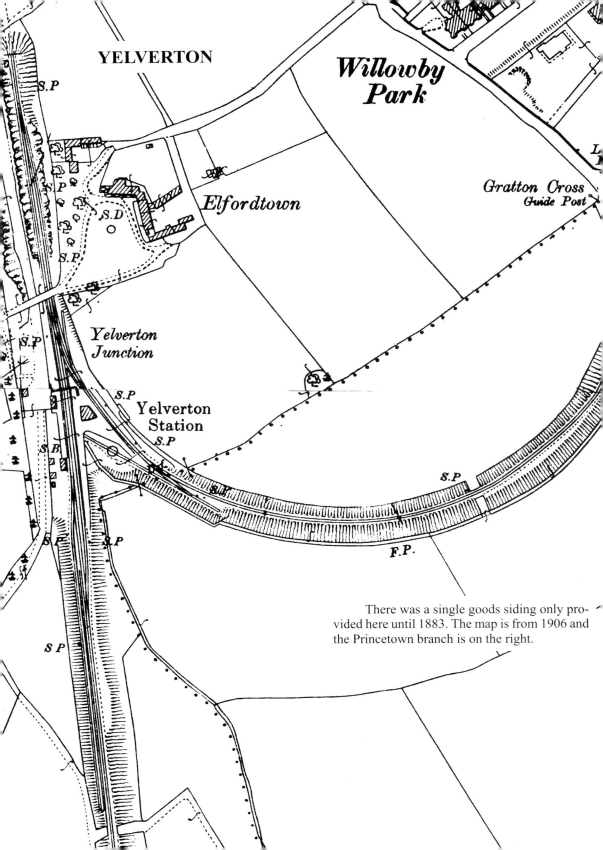

YELVERTON

*Willowby Park*

*Elfordtown*

Gratton Cross
Guide Post

S.P

S.P

S.D

S.P

Yelverton
Junction

S.P

S.P

Yelverton
Station

S.P

S.P

S.B

S.P

S.P

S.P

S.P

F.P.

S.P

There was a single goods siding only provided here until 1883. The map is from 1906 and
the Princetown branch is on the right.

43. Although the Princetown branch opened in 1883, this junction station was not opened until 1st May 1885. All branch trains ran to Horrabridge until that time. This postcard view features a train bound for Plymouth. (Lens of Sutton)

44. The branch had connections to both up and down lines, as shown, until 1933. After this time only the up line had a link, as seen in the picture after next. There was a good number of business travellers (now known as commuters) to Plymouth. (M.Dart coll.)

45. The branch curved away steeply towards Dartmoor from the end of the platform. The siding on the right led to the turntable - there was no goods yard. The photograph dates from 1945. After arrival, the branch engine would propel the train up the gradient, uncouple, retire to the siding and the guard would allow the coaches to roll back into the platform. (H.C.Casserley)

47. The hand worked turntable was 23ft 6ins in length and the building on the right was almost pentagonal in plan. No. 4410 is waiting to leave for Princetown on 5th July 1955. (R.C.Riley)

46. The station is at the summit of the route to Tavistock and no. 4542 is about to depart for that town and enter the 641yd long Yelverton Tunnel. This is on a down gradient of 1 in 110, lengths of 1 in 60 down following to Horrabridge. The local population amounted to about 2700 souls when the line closed. (H.C.Casserley)

48. No. 3675 had an autocoach and a van in tow as it approached the down platform on 17th August 1955. The signal box had 35 levers and was in use until 4th May 1959. It also worked the branch points seen in picture no. 45. (R.E.Toop)

49. The branch closed in March 1956 and the connection on the left was removed on 28th April 1957. This picture from June 1956 shows no. 4583 attached to a boat train luggage van. A down refuge siding was provided near the rear of the train. (J.W.T.House/C.L.Caddy)

50. The up loop (left) was taken out of use on 4th May 1959, when the signal box (right) ceased to function. There had been a staff of eight in 1931-34. The site now forms part of a private nature reserve, the buildings having been demolished in 1964. (C.L.Caddy)

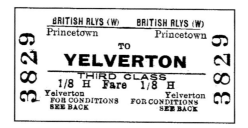

| Yelverton | 1903 | 1913 | 1923 | 1933 |
|---|---|---|---|---|
| Passenger tickets issued | 42549 | 48018 | 39917 | 30418 |
| Season tickets issued | * | * | 438 | 203 |
| Parcels forwarded | 5699 | 9024 | 5000 | 4282 |

# PRINCETOWN BRANCH

## DOUSLAND

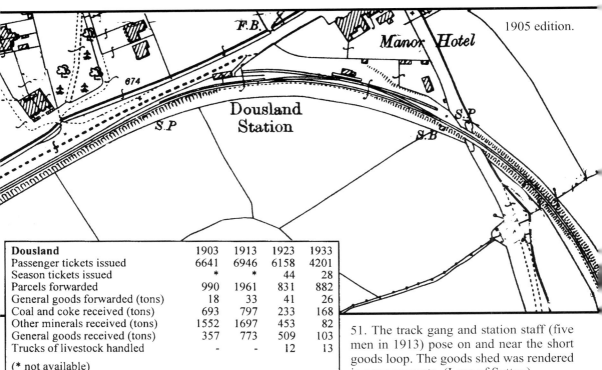

1905 edition.

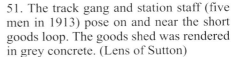

| Dousland | 1903 | 1913 | 1923 | 1933 |
|---|---|---|---|---|
| Passenger tickets issued | 6641 | 6946 | 6158 | 4201 |
| Season tickets issued | * | * | 44 | 28 |
| Parcels forwarded | 990 | 1961 | 831 | 882 |
| General goods forwarded (tons) | 18 | 33 | 41 | 26 |
| Coal and coke received (tons) | 693 | 797 | 233 | 168 |
| Other minerals received (tons) | 1552 | 1697 | 453 | 82 |
| General goods received (tons) | 357 | 773 | 509 | 103 |
| Trucks of livestock handled | - | - | 12 | 13 |
| (* not available) | | | | |

51. The track gang and station staff (five men in 1913) pose on and near the short goods loop. The goods shed was rendered in grey concrete. (Lens of Sutton)

52. Centre is the signal box which was situated at the east end of the platform close to the loop points. It had a gate wheel and was reduced to a ground frame in 1915, when a new box was built on the platform. (Lens of Sutton)

53. The signal box was a block post, with electric train staff. It had 14 levers, one of which was spare, and carried a nameboard bearing DOUSLAND BARN. This view is from the 1930s; buses took most of the passengers after they started in 1931. (Stations UK)

54. The little station was recorded on its last day of use. The yard was used by a coal merchant from 1957 to 1971, after which it was used for gardens of new houses. The station building was adapted as a dwelling and still stands. (N.Simmons)

GWR Appendix for 1939.

### Excursion Trains to Dousland.

With a view to avoiding the use of two engines on Excursion trains between Yelverton and Dousland, such trains as require assistance between the points named will be timed to reach Yelverton to connect with one of the ordinary trains, and the following instructions must be carried out:—

The ordinary Branch train will be drawn up to the Yelverton Branch Starting Signal. The Excursion train, which must not exceed eight eight-wheel coaches, will then draw ahead in the direction of Horrabridge over the points leading to the Branch line, and be steadily backed on to the Branch train. Both trains will then be coupled together, and when this is done, the combined trains may be started. The Enginemen must carry out the pre-scribed rules, and be careful to start their engines at one and the same time, in the manner described in Rule 133 and in the General Appendix.

On arrival at Dousland, the combined train must be stopped with the coaches of the ordinary Branch train at the platform, and while the passengers are alighting, the Branch train must be uncoupled by the Branch Guard, and as soon as the passengers have alighted, and the Train Staff for the onward section has been handed to the Engine-man, the Branch train will proceed on its journey to Princetown. The Train Staff must be retained by the Engine-man of the Excursion train, which will be slowly propelled to the platform, and when the passengers have alighted, the empty coaches will return to Yelverton after the Staff has been placed in the instrument, and "Line clear" obtained from Yelverton for the empty train with the Train Staff, as usual.

While the Excursion train is standing at Dousland platform, the Loop points must be set for the Loop except when it is necessary to place the level crossing gates across the line to permit vehicles to pass over them.

Loaded Passenger trains may be banked in the rear from Yelverton to Dousland in accordance with the instruc-tions on page 145 of the General Appendix, which must be strictly adhered to. Distance 1 mile 51 chains. Gradient rising all the way. Ruling gradient 1 in 40.

The arrangement outlined above will also apply in the case of empty coaches going to Dousland to work the return Excursions at night.

# BURRATOR & SHEEPSTOR HALT

55. Burrator Reservoir, which provides much of Plymouth's water, was nearby and this was an attraction for ramblers. It had been built in 1893-98 but the halt did not open until 4th February 1924. It is seen in 1955. (L.W.Rowe)

56. The water level was raised in 1928, work starting in 1924. At least the workers had a halt nearby for that period of construction. Note that electric lighting was provided. Nos 4583 and 4568 are seen with the 4.0pm from Princetown on the last day of branch operation, 3rd March 1956. (S.C.Nash)

# INGRA TOR HALT

57. The altitude and exposure to wind caused snow drifts in cuttings on several occasions. This scene was recorded in March 1891, when the crew and six passengers were trapped overnight, the latter spending two nights on board. The train was immobile for eight days. Eggworthy siding was nearby. (Plymouth Library)

58. Desolate rock-strewn countryside or dense mist greets passengers at this height on Dartmoor. No. 4410 is making its descent on 21st August 1954. The sign warns dog owners to beware of snakes. The oil-lit halt opened on 2nd March 1936. (R.S.Carpenter)

59. The cold air on 1st March 1956 makes otherwise invisible steam leaks a hazard for the photographer. The wet rails will not help no. 4568 to start the 9.04 from Yelverton on the 1 in 72 gradient. (R.M.Casserley)

# KING TOR PLATFORM

60. February 1947 brought exceptionally severe weather and 0-6-0PT no. 1990 conveyed sailors from Devonport in three brake vans to clear a blocked cutting in an attempt to reopen the branch. (Western Morning News)

61. In better weather, the timber-built platform was a pleasant place to alight for a hike. It came into use on 2nd April 1928 and is seen in 1955. Quarry sidings were to be found downhill from this location. They were named Swell Tor and Royal Oak, but the latter was lifted in 1924. (R.C.Riley)

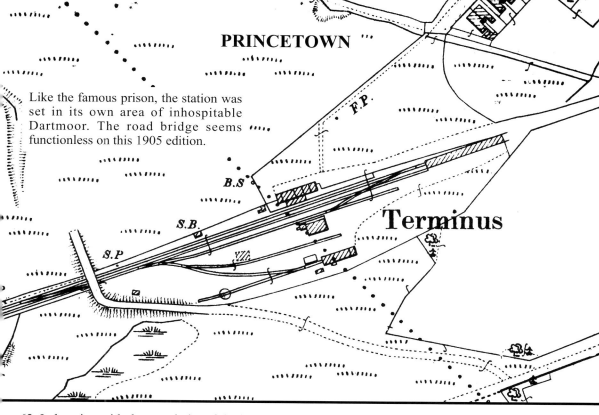

**PRINCETOWN**

Like the famous prison, the station was set in its own area of inhospitable Dartmoor. The road bridge seems functionless on this 1905 edition.

FP.

B.S

S.B.

S.P

Terminus

62. In keeping with the remainder of the branch, the approach to the terminus was sharply curved. The station is beyond the bridge at an altitude of 1373ft above sea level. The railway cottages are in view. (Lens of Sutton)

63. A view towards the end of the line includes the carriage shed, which was demolished in 1928. Its dark interior shows in the centre of the picture. The three attached railwaymans cottages and the station masters house are seen fully in the next picture. (Lens of Sutton)

64. The 23ft 6ins turntable is between the camera and the signal box, while the sidings seem well filled with wagons. Inmates of His Majesty's Prison ceased to be conveyed on the branch after about 1930, except during and soon after World War II. It was more expedient to use the SR route to Tavistock, and then onward by road. (Lens of Sutton)

55. Few GWR terminal stations looked like prisons and were devoid of doors and signboards on the road side. Some details of the goods shed are also evident. There was a staff of five on commercial matters in the first quarter of the 20th century. (Lens of Sutton)

56. The water column and a LNER wagon (usually lettered simply NE) are included in this 1936 panorama. An exceptional and record 1135 tons of coal had been received that year. There was a siding in the foreground in the 1920s, serving a timber depot. (W.A.Camwell)

| Princetown | 1903 | 1913 | 1923 | 1933 |
|---|---|---|---|---|
| Passenger tickets issued | 11535 | 12679 | 10665 | 10715 |
| Season tickets issued | * | * | 70 | 102 |
| Parcels forwarded | 6218 | 9213 | 4921 | 5266 |
| General goods forwarded (tons) | 351 | 426 | 226 | 190 |
| Coal and coke received (tons) | 4007 | 2627 | 625 | 1819 |
| Other minerals received (tons) | 613 | 560 | 740 | 3524 |
| General goods received (tons) | 2970 | 3213 | 2718 | 1074 |
| Trucks of livestock handled | 19 | 33 | 28 | 9 |

(* not available)

67. The 4400 class served the branch almost exclusively for over 50 years. No. 4402 is on the 3.55pm departure on 4th September 1947. One coach was more than adequate for most of the year. (S.C.Nash)

68. The goods office is on the left as no. 4410 runs round its train in July 1955, while a solitary passenger approaches. All the buildings had been demolished by 1960. There was a 5-ton crane in the yard, with a 2-ton one in the goods shed. (R.C.Riley)

69. The signal box had a 14-lever frame and was cement rendered, as were all the other buildings. No. 4568 is leaving at 10.30am on 1st March 1956, two days before the last trains ran. (R.M.Casserley)

70. The roof-mounted water tank is evident on the locomotive shed, as a solitary wagon stands in the mist in the last week of operation . The first train left at 7.35am and the last arrived at 7.41pm. (R.M.Casserley)

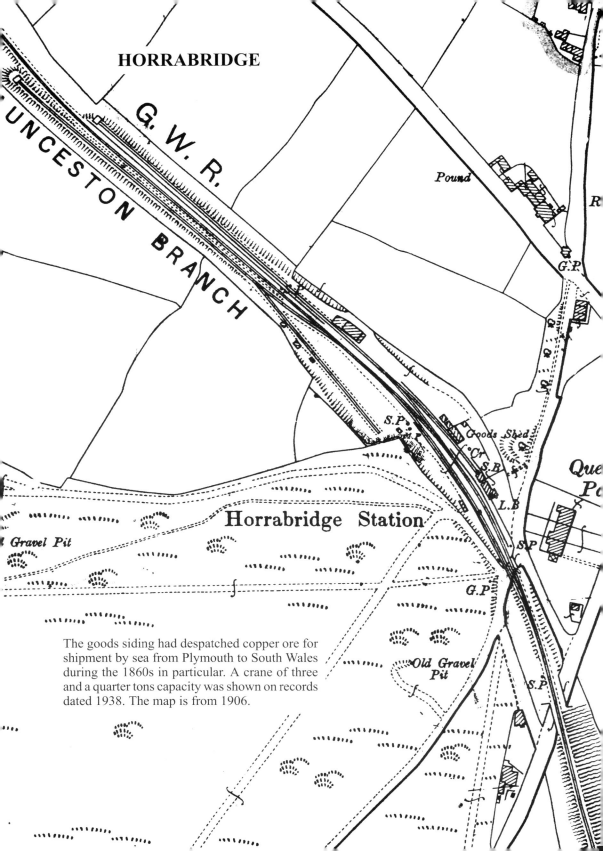

**HORRABRIDGE**

G. W. R.

LAUNCESTON BRANCH

Pound

Horrabridge Station

Gravel Pit

The goods siding had despatched copper ore for shipment by sea from Plymouth to South Wales during the 1860s in particular. A crane of three and a quarter tons capacity was shown on records dated 1938. The map is from 1906.

Old Gravel Pit

Goods Shed

S.P.

Que Po

G.P.

71. A northward view includes the original type of track which had longitudinal timbers tied together with transoms. These had all been shortened during the gauge changing weekend. This was the junction for Princetown from 1883 to 1885. (Lens of Sutton)

72. A similar panorama in the 1950s reveals that little had changed. This picture was taken from the site of the level crossing which had been closed on 5th March 1952. Both water columns are included, as is the roadway to the single siding goods yard. Another siding had been laid on the other side of the running lines in 1905. (Lens of Sutton)

73. There was a local population of about 1400 at the time of closure. This was not far off when no. 4555 was recorded with a train from Plymouth on 23rd June 1962. The site was cleared in 1979 to make way for industrial buildings. (M.J.Messenger)

| Horrabridge | 1903 | 1913 | 1923 | 1933 |
|---|---|---|---|---|
| Passenger tickets issued | 24763 | 26570 | 25715 | 24281 |
| Season tickets issued | * | * | 320 | 357 |
| Parcels forwarded | 4848 | 7404 | 4926 | 3549 |
| General goods forwarded (tons) | 600 | 510 | 258 | 125 |
| Coal and coke received (tons) | 2660 | 2074 | 722 | 4639 |
| Other minerals received (tons) | 3781 | 2060 | 744 | 76 |
| General goods received (tons) | 720 | 4493 | 3543 | 4100 |
| Trucks of livestock handled | 73 | 80 | 8 | - |
| (* not available) | | | | |

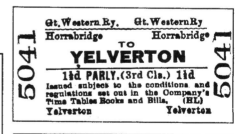

Gt. Western Ry.    Gt. Western Ry
Horrabridge        Horrabridge
TO
YELVERTON
1½d PARLY.(3rd Cls.) 1½d
Issued subject to the conditions and
regulations set out in the Company's
Time Tables Books and Bills.    (HL)
Yelverton                        Yelverton
5041

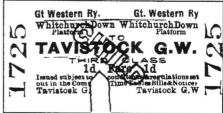

Gt Western Ry.    Gt. Western Ry
Whitchurch Down   Whitchurch Down
Platform          Platform
TO
TAVISTOCK G.W.
THIRD CLASS
1d Fare 1d
Issued subject to   conditions & regulations set
out in the Com      Time Tables Bills & Notices
Tavistock G.        Tavistock G,W
1725

# NORTH OF HORRABRIDGE

74. Northbound trains first crossed the short Magpie Viaduct, which had been rebuit in stone in 1902. Next was the 367yd long Grenofen or Walkham Viaduct, seen here. Reconstruction of the 15 spans was undertaken in 1910. (M.Dart coll.)

# WHITCHURCH DOWN PLATFORM

75. After passing through the 374 yd long Grenofen Tunnel under the A386, trains reached Whitchurch, now a suburb of Tavistock. The gas-lit platform came into use on 1st September 1906. Beyond it, there had been a siding on the east side for loading copper ore from Wheal Crelake Mine. (Lens of Sutton)

# TAVISTOCK SOUTH

The 1906 survey shows a private siding to a saw mill and reveals the
convenient proximity of the cattle market.

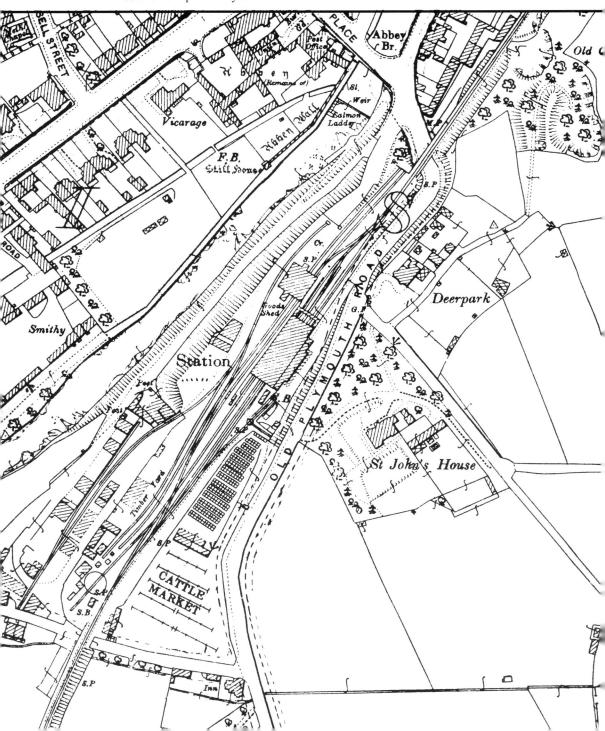

76. Although severely damaged by fire in 1887, the overall roof was repaired and was photographed in about 1939, looking north. The buildings were built of timber and were reconstructed in stone after the fire. The station was a terminus for trains from Plymouth from 1859 to 1865. (Stations UK)

77. The suffix SOUTH was added on 26th September 1949. An autotrain was photographed in the up platform, ten years later. The centre road was not used by passenger trains. (J.H.Aston)

78. Although not sharp, this picture of the 3.5pm from Plymouth on 4th November 1961 is included as it shows the water tank, the line to the 45ft turntable and the former "B" Box, which had served as a Signal & Telegraph Department store and office for over 50 years. (L.W.Crosier)

79. Ex-GWR 0-6-0PT no. 6430 has just moved forward for water after arrival on 23rd June 1962. Over half the trains from Plymouth terminated here in the final years, more in earlier days. (M.J.Messenger)

80. Later the same day, no. 5544 arrives with freight from Launceston. It will have first passed the 1921 Pitts Cleave Quarry sidings where roadstone and railway ballast was loaded. Goods inward at the yard included coal, fertilisers and feedstuffs; outwards notably were wool, pit-props and granite. (M.J.Messenger)

A 00049

BRITISH RAILWAYS (W)
Issued at Tavistock South

Receipt for
EXCESS FARE

7 d

H

MARY TAVY
TO
TAVISTOCK SOUTH

| Tavistock | 1903 | 1913 | 1923 | 1933 |
|---|---|---|---|---|
| Passenger tickets issued | 44664 | 79532 | 58446 | 53591 |
| Season tickets issued | * | * | 281 | 323 |
| Parcels forwarded | 20331 | 21483 | 20170 | 21944 |
| General goods forwarded (tons) | 1272 | 2524 | 1260 | 472 |
| Coal and coke received (tons) | 7855 | 7552 | 1564 | 3780 |
| Other minerals received (tons) | 5193 | 1741 | 1475 | 794 |
| General goods received (tons) | 3169 | 7815 | 8719 | 6777 |
| Trucks of livestock handled | 412 | 544 | 279 | 198 |
| (* not available) | | | | |

81. On the last day of passenger services (29th December 1962), the final train from Plymouth should have been the 8.40pm. Owing to very severe blizzards and low temperatures, the 6.20 left 72 minutes late and eventually arrived, after heroic work by staff, at 12.25am. It was soon immobilised by ice and police helped serve tea at 3.0am; the photograph was taken at 6.25am. The 7.10pm southbound departure had become stuck at Bickleigh and passengers spent the night in the signal box, as there was no steam left to heat the train. (M.Dart)

82. The entrance was on the up side and was photographed in July 1963. The population was over 6000 but their interest in using the trains diminished after ten years of petrol rationing ended in 1950. During the bombing of Plymouth, crowds arrived every evening and left in the morning. (Lens of Sutton)

83. On the right of this 1963 picture is the loading dock and crane, which could lift eleven and a half tons. There was a siding for the gasworks south of the station from 1938 to 1957. The yard had been very busy towards the end of World War II, owing to a large number of Army camps in the area. (C.L.Caddy)

*Tavistock North is illustrated in*
**Exeter to Tavistock** *and*
**Tavistock to Plymouth**
*(Middleton Press)*

84. Goods traffic ceased on 7th September 1964, the 36-lever signal box having closed on 27th July of that year. Taken in October, this photograph includes the once busy cattle dock and the weigh-house with pitched roof, next to the curved-roof lamp hut. An industrial estate now occupies most of the site. (C.L.Caddy)

# MARY TAVY AND BLACKDOWN

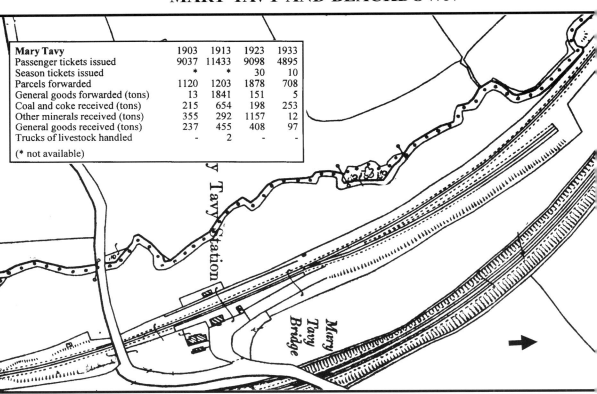

| Mary Tavy | 1903 | 1913 | 1923 | 1933 |
|---|---|---|---|---|
| Passenger tickets issued | 9037 | 11433 | 9098 | 4895 |
| Season tickets issued | * | * | 30 | 10 |
| Parcels forwarded | 1120 | 1203 | 1878 | 708 |
| General goods forwarded (tons) | 13 | 1841 | 151 | 5 |
| Coal and coke received (tons) | 215 | 654 | 198 | 253 |
| Other minerals received (tons) | 355 | 292 | 1157 | 12 |
| General goods received (tons) | 237 | 455 | 408 | 97 |
| Trucks of livestock handled | - | 2 | - | - |
| (* not available) | | | | |

The local population was 763 in 1961. Staffing ceased and the short siding was closed on 11th August 1941. The map was published in 1906 and the suffix "Blackdown" was added in the following year.

85. An up freight train obscures the single siding in about 1939. The loop and signal box had been out of use since 1892, having been little used since LSWR trains had been withdrawn in 1890. A ground frame shelter can be seen on the disused down platform. (Stations UK)

86. A lone passenger waits to join the 2.5pm Launceston to Plymouth train on 23rd June 1962; no. 5541 is in charge. The former LSWR route is in the cutting which appears level with the ridge tiles of the railway cottages, which still stand. (J.J.Smith)

87. Recorded near Mary Tavy on 10th May 1961 was no. 5541 with the 3.5pm from Plymouth. When the LSWR completed its parallel double track, it opened a station at Brentor, about two miles to the north of the GWR station. (S.C.Nash)

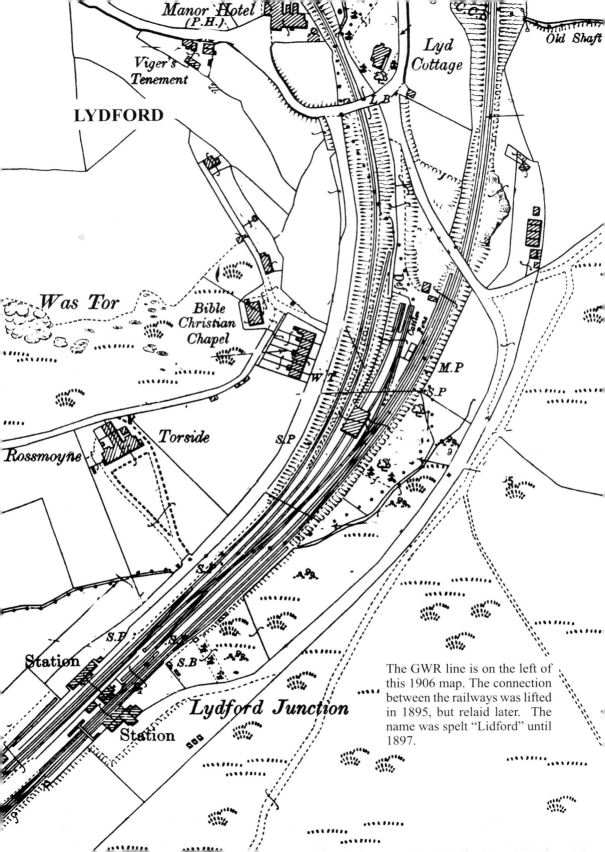

Manor Hotel
(P.H.)

Viger's
Tenement

Lyd
Cottage

Old Shaft

LYDFORD

Was Tor

Bible
Christian
Chapel

M.P

S.P

W

S.P

Torside

Rossmoyne

S.B

Station

S.B

Lydford Junction

Station

The GWR line is on the left of
this 1906 map. The connection
between the railways was lifted
in 1895, but relaid later.  The
name was spelt "Lidford" until
1897.

88. The nearest of the two parallel stations is that of the GWR. That company's signal box is on the right, while the great mass of granite that forms Dartmoor is in the background. The buildings were incorrectly coloured on the original postcard. (M.Dart coll.)

89. The ex-GWR station is on the left; that company laid a siding on the alignment of the one in the foreground in 1886. Another was laid parallel to it and a third was provided straight ahead. This small goods yard was closed in 1917. (J.J.Smith)

90. The connecting line between the two systems was disused between 1915 and 1935 but restored in the Summer of 1943, as a wartime measure. Three sidings (centre) and five more to the east (left) were laid at this time. No. 5544 is entering the loop with a train from Plymouth. (J.J.Smith)

91. A Launceston to Plymouth train departs, as one arrives from Okehampton. There was a footbridge over the Southern Region lines but not over those of the Western. No trace of these buildings now remains. (J.J.Smith)

92. No. 4567 approaches the station with a train from Launceston, having passed an antique tapered wooden signal post. Pictures 89 to 92 were all taken in 1962. The sidings ceased to be used in the following year. (S.C.Nash)

93. The LSWR and GWR provided staff for their separate stations until March 1914, after which the former staffed both. Their uniforms showed both company's lettering however. This 1964 photograph features the then disused ex-GWR platforms. (C.L.Caddy)

94. Pictured in 1966, the booking office continued in use until May 1968, when the alternative route to Plymouth closed. The signal box opened on 8th January 1917; it had one lever frame behind these windows and another near the windows seen in the previous picture. (Wessex coll.)

| Lydford | 1903 | 1913 | 1923 | 1933 |
|---|---|---|---|---|
| Passenger tickets issued | 5872 | 4823 | 4278 | 2417 |
| Season tickets issued | * | * | 17 | 4 |
| Parcels forwarded | 881 | 1290 | 637 | 426 |
| General goods forwarded (tons) | 56 | 28 | 41 | 4 |
| Coal and coke received (tons) | 157 | 181 | 4 | 30 |
| Other minerals received (tons) | 30 | 1387 | 19 | 79 |
| General goods received (tons) | 84 | 93 | 168 | 62 |
| Trucks of livestock handled | 18 | 19 | 9 | 5 |
| (* not available) | | | | |

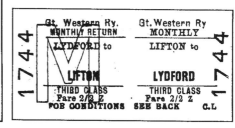

95. The goods shed evident in the previous picture had initially been used for the transfer of merchandise between wagons of different gauges. North of it were cattle pens to serve the same purpose. Remarkably they were still in place in 1966 and showed their original owners' differing styles of construction. The goods yard closed on 7th September 1964. (Wessex coll.)

*Other views of this station can be seen in pictures 95 to 102 in our* **Exeter to Tavistock** *album.*

# LIDDATON HALT

96. The all wooden construction was opened to traffic on 4th April 1938. Up trains had to climb at 1 in 55 when departing for Lydford. (Lens of Sutton)

| Coryton | 1903 | 1913 | 1923 | 1933 |
|---|---|---|---|---|
| Passenger tickets issued | 7469 | 7527 | 6867 | 3508 |
| Season tickets issued | * | * | 26 | 10 |
| Parcels forwarded | 4168 | 6013 | 11362 | 10309 |
| General goods forwarded (tons) | 133 | 683 | 965 | 91 |
| Coal and coke received (tons) | 1123 | 173 | 76 | 177 |
| Other minerals received (tons) | 125 | 241 | 411 | 1937 |
| General goods received (tons) | 1116 | 1574 | 1623 | 946 |
| Trucks of livestock handled | 8 | 55 | 39 | 25 |
| (* not available) | | | | |

# CORYTON

97. A class 3521 4-4-0 proceeds towards Launceston with what is probably a special train. The complicated scissors crossing was replaced by a trailing connection in the up direction in about 1934. The ground frame hut and loading dock are visible. (M.Dart coll.)

1906 survey

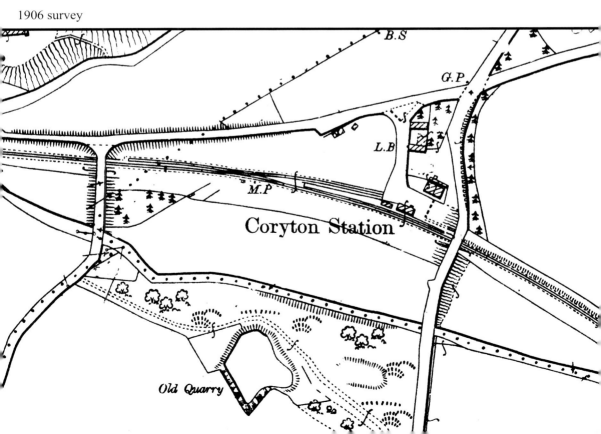

98. Large tonnages of manganese had been loaded here in the 1870s, but traffic was very light thereafter. The parcels shed (left) was adequate for the limited business offering. Staffing ceased in 1959. (M.Dart coll.)

99. The Plymouth Railway Circle operated a railtour on 11th December 1965; it enabled the participants to note that the track had been relaid with concrete sleepers. The building has been incorporated into a modern dwelling. (C.L.Caddy)

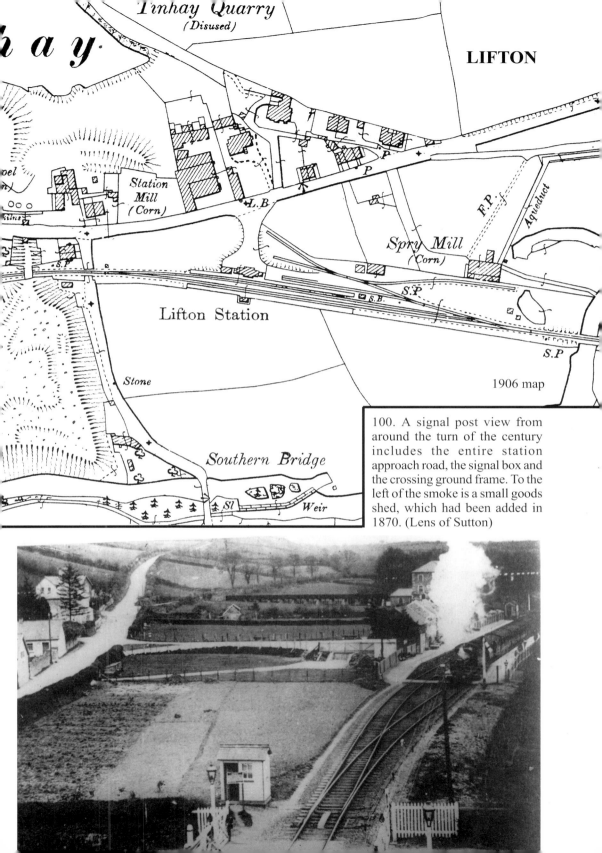

Tinhay Quarry
*(Disused)*

ha y.

**LIFTON**

Station
Mill
*(Corn)*

L.B.

Spry Mill
*(Corn)*

F.P.

Aqueduct

S.P.

Lifton Station

S.B.

S.P.

S.P.

Stone

1906 map

Southern Bridge

Sl

Weir

100. A signal post view from around the turn of the century includes the entire station approach road, the signal box and the crossing ground frame. To the left of the smoke is a small goods shed, which had been added in 1870. (Lens of Sutton)

101. A similar but later view includes the Ambrosia factory, which was established in 1917 on GWR land. Its celebrated output has been canned rice puddings. In the background is a corn mill which had a private siding. Dairy buildings now cover the entire site. (M.Dart coll.)

| Lifton | 1903 | 1913 | 1923 | 1933 |
|---|---|---|---|---|
| Passenger tickets issued | 12018 | 12290 | 13086 | 7333 |
| Season tickets issued | * | * | 44 | 56 |
| Parcels forwarded | 3386 | 10240 | 8770 | 9835 |
| General goods forwarded (tons) | 606 | 392 | 800 | 869 |
| Coal and coke received (tons) | 764 | 376 | 10 | 1316 |
| Other minerals received (tons) | 150 | 457 | 1355 | 445 |
| General goods received (tons) | 3202 | 1820 | 4700 | 9856 |
| Trucks of livestock handled | 28 | 112 | 76 | 69 |

(* not available)

102. No. 4592 obscures the main building, which was of a similar design to that at Coryton. The arch in the background once carried a narrow gauge line to Tinhay Quarry. The inset door of the leading coach indicates that it is one of an extra-wide batch built for London-Plymouth boat trains. The date is June 1956.
(J.W.T.House/C.L.Caddy)

103. There were 17 levers in the box but the single line staff instruments were situated in the booking office. The six-ton goods crane is visible, as are vans and milk tanks in the waiting passenger train. These had just been added to the train seen in the previous picture. The local population was 840 when the line closed. (J.W.T.House/C.L.Caddy)

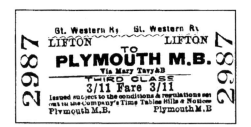

104. The signal box was used as a ground frame from September 1964 and most signals were removed. The headboard gives the reason for no. 41283 appearing with a rare passenger train on 5th September 1965. While the Marsh Mills - Launceston route was closed entirely at the end of 1962 (except for Tavistock South Goods), the Lydford - Lifton section was retained for milk traffic and worked by a locomotive from Okehampton Shed. However, this part was closed on 7th September 1964 and the Lifton - Launceston length was reopened to handle the Ambrosia output. All traffic ceased on 28th February 1966. (S.C.Nash)

# EAST OF LAUNCESTON

105. The route passed under the ex-LSWR Padstow line on the approach to Launceston, about half a mile from the terminus. No. 5569 was pictured on 1st July 1961. A connecting line was available from 22nd September 1943 and was used for regular passenger trains from 30th June 1952. (A.G.Thorpe)

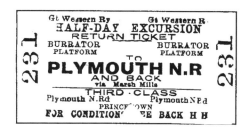

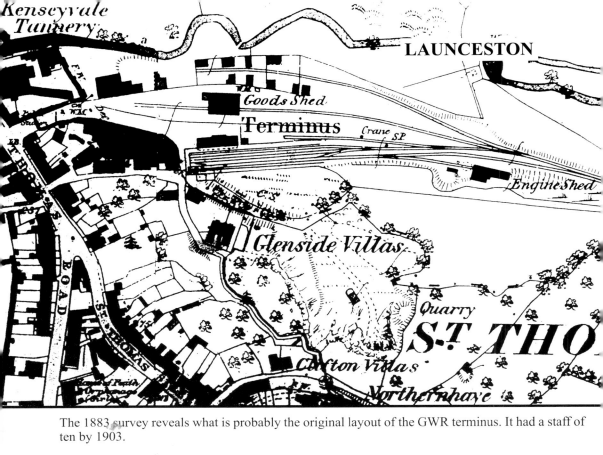

The 1883 survey reveals what is probably the original layout of the GWR terminus. It had a staff of ten by 1903.

106. The GWR sidings are nearest to us in this southward view, the station being largely obscured by the tree on the right. A siding east of the station was provided for Cawdron Quarry betwen 1865 and 1894, and again later. The castle and church were (and are) tourist attractions. (Lens of Sutton)

107. Two photographs from about 1939 show full passenger facilities such as seats and lighting, which was by gas. The upward extension of the front wall is believed to have been part of a plan for an overall roof, similar to the one provided at Tavistock. (Stations UK)

The 1906 edition includes the LSWR station on the Okehampton - Padstow line. The GWR tracks had been rearranged in 1894. Neither turntable pits are shown. The two stations were termed "North" and "South" from 18th June 1951.

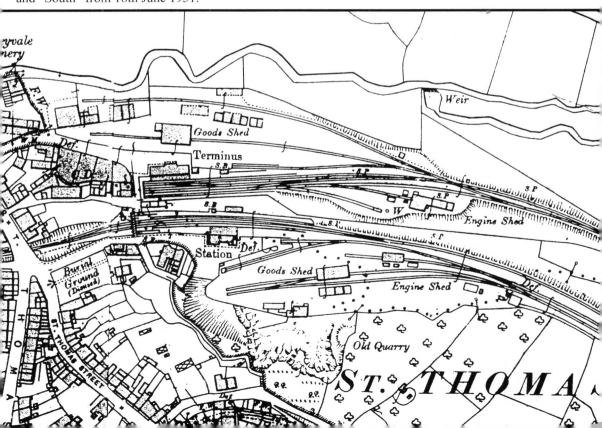

108. The seven and a half ton goods crane can be seen peeping over the middle van. As part of BR's rationalisation programme, all passenger trains were transferred to the adjacent station after 30th June 1952. However, the 10.15am departure on 9th May 1956 was from this platform, as the Royal Train was occupying one of the through lines. (Stations UK)

———————▶

109. Looking east from the end of the platform in 1950, we see the ground frame, engine shed and turntable, which was 45ft in length. One class 4500 2-6-2T was allocated here until the end of 1962. (D.Clayton)

———————▶

110. A 1959 view shows two container wagons standing at the loading dock, with the goods shed behind them. This contained a 2-ton crane. There is evidence of platform lengthening on the right; the other one probably was never used by a passenger. (Lens of Sutton)

111. The station building was used for freight traffic until the yard closed on 28th February 1966. The Southern Region station was in use until 3rd October of that year, but for passengers only. (R.S.Carpenter)

| Launceston | 1903 | 1913 | 1923 | 1933 |
|---|---|---|---|---|
| Passenger tickets issued | 18215 | 18107 | 18036 | 6512 |
| Season tickets issued | * | * | 47 | 18 |
| Parcels forwarded | 14492 | 19922 | 28557 | 25373 |
| General goods forwarded (tons) | 1244 | 1643 | 1348 | 345 |
| Coal and coke received (tons) | 2874 | 845 | 708 | 1715 |
| Other minerals received (tons) | 1261 | 1175 | 1311 | 4533 |
| General goods received (tons) | 5684 | 7832 | 8850 | 10198 |
| Trucks of livestock handled | 214 | 357 | 324 | 393 |
| (* not available) | | | | |

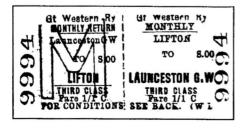

112. No. 4583 was photographed in June 1956 taking water after its 31 mile journey from Plymouth. The use of the through platforms facilitated the transfer of parcels, as well as making an easier change for passengers. (J.W.T.House/C.L.Caddy)

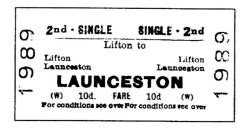

113. After taking water, branch engines would run round the coaches and transfer them to the up platform. This is the 5.40pm to Plymouth on 26th May 1958. As at Lydford, the signal box was designed to serve both the LSWR and the GWR. It did so from 31st December 1916. (J.N.Faulkner)

114. No. 4555 waits to depart for Plymouth on 23rd June 1962. The lattice iron footbridge in the background was built by the LSWR. The population of the town had dropped to about 4500 at the time of closure. (M.J.Messenger)

More pictures of this station can be enjoyed in our **Branch Line to Padstow.**

115. The tank wagon and the ground frame hut have been seen already in picture no. 109. The locomotive from picture no. 104 proceeds towards the former GWR station with the special train on 5th September 1965. (M.J.Messenger)

116. The GWR side of the signal box was photographed on 11th December 1965. Its point rodding and signal wires can be seen on the right of the next picture. (C.L.Caddy)

117. The railtour illustrated in photograph no. 99 visited the terminus. The door on the goods shed had been designed for broad gauge wagons. The site of the station is now occupied by an industrial estate. The middle siding had been taken out in 1964. (C.L.Caddy)

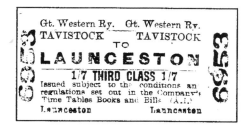

Gt. Western Ry.    Gt. Western Ry.
TAVISTOCK        TAVISTOCK
TO
LAUNCESTON
1/7 THIRD CLASS 1/7
Issued subject to the conditions an
regulations set out in the Company's
Time Tables Books and Bills (A.I.)
Launceston        Launceston

6953

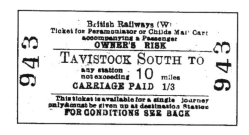

British Railways (W)
Ticket for Perambulator or Childs Mail Cart
accompanying a Passenger
OWNER'S RISK
TAVISTOCK SOUTH TO
any station
not exceeding    10    miles
CARRIAGE PAID    1/3
This ticket is available for a single journey
only & must be given up at destination Station
FOR CONDITIONS SEE BACK

943

# LAUNCESTON STEAM RAILWAY

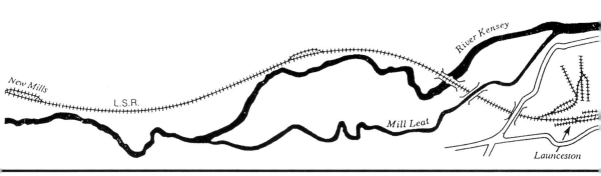

The one foot eleven and a half inch gauge line was established in 1983 and a demonstration length came into use on 26th December. Progressive openings followed until the two and a half miles to New Mills was completed for traffic to start on 27th May 1995.

118. The entire route was laid on the trackbed of the LSWR, commencing immediately west of the original station. Hunslet 0-4-0ST *Lilian* of 1883 was pictured in March 1995 at Launceston, prior to running round. The siding on the platform is for winter storage of coaches under the canopy, which came from Tavistock North. (V.Mitchell)

119. At the west end of the loop at Launceston is a finely ornamented running shed. The locomotive fleet includes four other former Welsh slate quarry engines: *Covertcoat, Dorothea, Sybil* and *Velinheli*. The coach formerly ran on the Inny Valley Railway. (V.Mitchell)

120. New Mills was provided with this stylish waiting shelter in 1997 and was photographed on 10th May 1998, with *Lilian* in attendance. The coach is a replica of the one built in the 1890s by Milnes of Birkenhead for use on the ill-fated Plynlimmon and Hafan Railway in Central Wales. The replica was built at Launceston during the early 1990s. This gentle steam excursion is a fine way to kindle memories of a bygone era of rural transport. (Mrs K.Bowman)

# MP Middleton Press

Easebourne Lane, Midhurst, West Sussex. GU29 9AZ Tel: 01730 813169 Fax: 01730 812601

*... WRITE OR PHONE FOR OUR LATEST LIST ...*

## BRANCH LINES
Branch Line to Allhallows
Branch Lines to Alton
Branch Lines around Ascot
Branch Line to Ashburton
Branch Lines around Bodmin
Branch Line to Bude
Branch Lines around Canterbury
Branch Line to Cheddar
Branch Lines to East Grinstead
Branch Line to Effingham Junction
Branch Line to Fairford
Branch Line to Hawkhurst
Branch Line to Hayling
Branch Line to Horsham
Branch Line to Ilfracombe
Branch Line to Kingswear
Branch Lines to Launceston & Princetown
Branch Lines to Longmoor
Branch Line to Lyme Regis
Branch Line to Lynton
Branch Lines around Midhurst
Branch Line to Minehead
Branch Lines to Newport (IOW)
Branch Line to Padstow
Branch Lines around Plymouth
Branch Lines around Portmadoc 1923-46
Branch Lines around Porthmadog 1954-94
Branch Lines to Seaton & Sidmouth
Branch Line to Selsey
Branch Lines around Sheerness
Branch Line to Southwold
Branch Line to Tenterden
Branch Lines to Torrington
Branch Lines to Tunbridge Wells
Branch Line to Upwell
Branch Lines around Wimborne
Branch Lines around Wisbech

## SOUTH COAST RAILWAYS
Ashford to Dover
Brighton to Eastbourne
Chichester to Portsmouth
Dover to Ramsgate
Hastings to Ashford
Portsmouth to Southampton
Ryde to Ventnor
Worthing to Chichester

## SOUTHERN MAIN LINES
Bromley South to Rochester
Charing Cross to Orpington
Crawley to Littlehampton
Dartford to Sittingbourne
East Croydon to Three Bridges
Epsom to Horsham
Exeter to Barnstaple
Exeter to Tavistock
Faversham to Dover
Haywards Heath to Seaford
London Bridge to East Croydon
Orpington to Tonbridge
Swanley to Ashford
Tavistock to Plymouth
Victoria to East Croydon
Waterloo to Windsor
Waterloo to Woking
Woking to Portsmouth

Woking to Southampton
Yeovil to Exeter

## COUNTRY RAILWAY ROUTES
Andover to Southampton
Bournemouth to Evercreech Jn.
Burnham to Evercreech Junction
Croydon to East Grinstead
Didcot to Winchester
Fareham to Salisbury
Frome to Bristol
Guildford to Redhill
Porthmadog to Blaenau
Reading to Basingstoke
Reading to Guildford
Redhill to Ashford
Salisbury to Westbury
Strood to Paddock Wood
Taunton to Barnstaple
Wenford Bridge to Fowey
Westbury to Bath
Woking to Alton
Yeovil to Dorchester

## GREAT RAILWAY ERAS
Ashford from Steam to Eurostar
Clapham Junction 50 years of change
Festiniog in the Fifties
Festiniog in the Sixties
Isle of Wight Lines 50 years of change

## LONDON SUBURBAN RAILWAYS
Caterham and Tattenham Corner
Charing Cross to Dartford
Clapham Jn. to Beckenham Jn.
Crystal Palace and Catford Loop
East London Line
Finsbury Park to Alexandra Palace
Holborn Viaduct to Lewisham
Kingston and Hounslow Loops
Lewisham to Dartford
Lines around Wimbledon
London Bridge to Addiscombe
North London Line
South London Line
West Croydon to Epsom
West London Line
Willesden Junction to Richmond
Wimbledon to Epsom

## STEAM PHOTOGRAPHERS
O.J.Morris's Southern Railways 1919-59

## STEAMING THROUGH
Steaming through Cornwall
Steaming through East Sussex
Steaming through the Isle of Wight
Steaming through Kent
Steaming through West Hants
Steaming through West Sussex

## TRAMWAY CLASSICS
Aldgate & Stepney Tramways
Barnet & Finchley Tramways
Bath Tramways
Bournemouth & Poole Tramways
Brighton's Tramways

Bristol's Tramways
Camberwell & W.Norwood Tramways
Clapham & Streatham Tramways
Dover's Tramways
East Ham & West Ham Tramways
Edgware and Willesden Tramways
Eltham & Woolwich Tramways
Embankment & Waterloo Tramways
Enfield & Wood Green Tramways
Exeter & Taunton Tramways
Gosport & Horndean Tramways
Greenwich & Dartford Tramways
Hampstead & Highgate Tramways
Hastings Tramways
Holborn & Finsbury Tramways
Ilford & Barking Tramways
Kingston & Wimbledon Tramways
Lewisham & Catford Tramways
Liverpool Tramways 1. Eastern Routes
Maidstone & Chatham Tramways
North Kent Tramways
Portsmouth's Tramways
Reading Tramways
Seaton & Eastbourne Tramways
Southampton Tramways
Southend-on-sea Tramways
Southwark & Deptford Tramways
Stamford Hill Tramways
Thanet's Tramways
Victoria & Lambeth Tramways
Waltham Cross & Edmonton Tramways
Walthamstow & Leyton Tramways
Wandsworth & Battersea Tramways

## TROLLEYBUS CLASSICS
Croydon Trolleybuses
Bournemouth Trolleybuses
Maidstone Trolleybuses
Reading Trolleybuses
Woolwich & Dartford Trolleybuses

## WATERWAY ALBUMS
Kent and East Sussex Waterways
London's Lost Route to the Sea
London to Portsmouth Waterway
Surrey Waterways
West Sussex Waterways

## MILITARY BOOKS
Battle over Sussex 1940
Blitz over Sussex 1941-42
Bombers over Sussex 1943-45
Bognor at War
Military Defence of West Sussex
Secret Sussex Resistance

## OTHER BOOKS
Betwixt Petersfield & Midhurst
Brickmaking in Sussex
Changing Midhurst
Garraway Father & Son
Index to all Stations
South Eastern & Chatham Railways
London Chatham & Dover Railway

## SOUTHERN RAILWAY VIDEO
War on the Line